T0356968

LADY SMITH

AKRON SERIES IN POETRY

AKRON SERIES IN POETRY
Mary Biddinger, Editor ·

Matthew Guenette, *Vasectomania*
Aimée Baker, *Doe*
Anne Barngrover, *Brazen Creature*
Emilia Phillips, *Empty Clip*
Emily Rosko, *Weather Inventions*
Caryl Pagel, *Twice Told*
Tyler Mills, *Hawk Parable*
Brittany Cavallaro, *Unhistorical*
Krystal Languell, *Quite Apart*
Oliver de la Paz, *The Boy in the Labyrinth*
Joshua Harmon, *The Soft Path*
Kimberly Quiogue Andrews, *A Brief History of Fruit*
Emily Corwin, *Sensorium*
Annah Browning, *Witch Doctrine*
Sean Shearer, *Red Lemons*
Heather Green, *No Other Rome*
Jennifer Moore, *Easy Does It*
Emilia Phillips, *Embouchure*
Aimee Seu, *Velvet Hounds*
Charles Jensen, *Instructions between Takeoff and Landing*
Heathen, *Outskirts*
Caryl Pagel, *Free Clean Fill Dirt*
Matthew Guenette, *Doom Scroll*
Carrie Oeding, *If I Could Give You a Line*
Jenny Sadre-Orafai, *Dear Outsiders*
Leslie Harrison, *Reck*
Anne Barngrover, *Everwhen*
Emily Corwin, *Marble Orchard*
Lena Khalaf Tuffaha, *Something about Living*
Emilia Phillips, *Nonbinary Bird of Paradise*
Jenny Sadre-Orafai, *Malak*
Jess Smith, *Lady Smith*

For a complete listing of titles published in the series,
go to www.uakron.edu/uapress/poetry

LADY SMITH

JESS SMITH

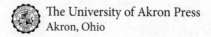
The University of Akron Press
Akron, Ohio

ISBN: 978-1-62922-303-2 (paper)
ISBN: 978-1-62922-304-9 (ePDF)
ISBN: 978-1-62922-305-6 (ePub)

A catalog record for this title is available from the Library of Congress.

∞ The paper used in this publication meets the minimum requirements of ANSI/NISO
z39.48–1992 (Permanence of Paper).

Cover image: Emily Starck, *Séoul*. Cover design by Amy Freels.

Lady Smith was designed and typeset in Minion with Helvetica titles by Amy Freels and
printed on fifty-five-pound natural.

Produced in conjunction with the University
of Akron Affordable Learning Initiative.
More information is available at
www.uakron.edu/affordablelearning

for my mother

Contents

III.

IV.

I.

We all forget things. That's what reminding is for.
—Patrick Bergin, *Sleeping with the Enemy*

Luster

Come gondola tongue, come narrow
passage, come lunar water vapor, nightfall
summoning the tide of him up and up

this begging shore, shining cliffs, his hard
hands a storm cloud in our shared sky,
synchronous orbit luring me to the thunder

of that body, silver satellite, the long milk he laps
from the canal of my spine, I'm all eyelash
and inhale, all estuary, all course and crushed

by the meteor of him, by the crater pretending
to be sea in the telescope's lone and limpid
eye, our only cries were answers, crawling

together through a light so clear it felt like wind,
like undertow you could—will—drown in.

No Other Appetite

The first time it was nightlight, lambent bloom,
the color of a bell. What sound is the shadow
of a man moving behind me? Not click, not

clap, something closer to applause but less
intact. The champagne I drink is a kind of chaos,
boiling cold in the mouth, prelude to oceanblue

blackout. I like life hot and quick, I like to blink
and miss it. His carnivore gaze, those lawless
canine irises (need I even say it?) should have been

red flags. But the tint of my life had brightened
to fluorescence, that wild cast of obliteration.
Morning and twilight burned the same white, both

of us gone feral and sunblind. The last time
it was whirling siren, bloodbath spun with sapphire.
My cobalt face, my blasted alabaster, my ghastly

human scraps. What color is the tongue
of a mother licking back to life her long-dead
cub? Indigo drips of ink spidering a hot glass

of water, surprise vermillion staining the back
of a young girl's newest dress. Nothing is enough
if you know how much you could have had.

Ode to StairMaster

Dear ladder to nowhere, dear Escher sketch
made manifest, thank you for allowing
my broke, hungover body to climb you,
an oblivious ascension, lifting the crescent
of my ass so it doesn't drag on the floor
like it feels like doing most days, mostly
when the wind carries a crisp apple scent
and in my other life I would have put on
his sweater, cranked the thermostat up
for the first time in the fall. Thank you,
StairMaster, you burned-down house
with only a staircase remaining, for letting me
pretend there are still bedrooms at the top
I can enter, children I need to wake in time
for pancakes. Thank you for making me hotter
in the loneliest way, for your attached screen
on which I watch endless loops of mindless
TV on silent, listening instead to sex-pop
songs with a thick beat, reminding myself
of the task underfoot, believing that if T-Pain
could see me, he'd be into it, maybe
serenade me from the top of the hill
I'll never reach. *Girl, it must be a crime*
to be as fine as you. Thank you, T-Pain.
Thank you, heavy bass. And thank you dear,
metal, gaping mouth whose teeth I scale
every day, whose black mechanics are just
what a heartless girl like me needs, you
who agree that the artless progression
toward improved-nudity-viewing is a worthy
pursuit. Dear body, dear ass, dear ever-harder
heart—I owe it all to you, StairMaster. Don't
give up on me now. I'm not even close.

Things People Say to Me After

A Cento

What did you do. How much had
you had. Has this happened
before. How many. I never
liked. I always knew. I'll find. I'll
kill. I know people. I know you
didn't. I know you never. This
won't. Everything will. With what
frequency. He would have. He would
have killed. Do you have
someone. Do you have
somewhere. Do you still live
in the residence with. Will you tell
the judge. I'm willing to pay
for your travel. Your medical. If. If
you just. You killed his. You seem
so. Seem very. Shh. I'm calling on
behalf of. We know how
these things. I'm going through
a separation, too. Do you need
a. Do you have a. Don't move
out while. It will make him. Don't
touch his. It was always. I am so sorry
I didn't. Inevitable. Are you
pregnant. How can you miss.
How can you still. Would you
describe. Just a few more. Stop
crying. Why won't you let
this. How could you. Who are
you to. Who do you think. To ruin
his. To hurt his. To make him.

Scold's Bridle

The house is too cold, my leash
icy leather. Even my tongue

can't warm this bit. And my tongue
is the hottest tongue. Feed me, when

will you feed me. What did I say
this time. You've taken

to recording me secretly.
Once, I at least had

some warning. I spy you
with my tilt-a-whirl eye:

Note-taking. Cock-thumbing.
You like me better

when I'm saran-wrapped. Best,
iron-branked. Feed me

birthday cake. This time
what did I say. Red rises

in the window though
it is not dawn. Match-spark casts

supple shadows: Fanged
wolf. Hanged witch. You stab

two candles into thick frosting.
I blow, and spit, and wish.

Vow

The sermon of the ocean: nothing lasts
that I wish dead. A light that looks like dawn
all day, that feels like the first hour
of winter, your hands demanding

their way into my sweater, the gust
of your blown mouth, how the breaking
waves strip the shore of its first skin, drag
their cage of larceny across whatever

has worked hard to crawl, on all
fours, away. Like the first time
I ever saw the Pacific, and you said
I told you it was bigger, the choking

foamy groan of high tide, God's jaw
unhinged and hungry. Your laughter slapped
against my skin, a signal that I, too,
should be happy. Of course the sea

has teeth. Of course we lie beside it
like a dare, starfish in our blood, limbs
that won't regrow, your hands at my
throat, isn't this romantic, isn't this

what I wanted? Isn't this how you always
end up—cold enough to know your blood
is hot, unsure enough to turn back
before you've even begun to run?

For Many Days After the Funeral, We Do Not Sleep

He's blacked out
every window, shattered

every lamp. One blinks
an unsteady pulse, groveling

on its broken shade.
He cannot find

enough to smash, rashing
my skin with a wreck

of handprints, the pink
of both nipples bite-

blackened. My hair
a handle, fingernails

twinkling with shards, blood
is not word enough

for the red
we've invited

into this room. All mouth, all
sound, all week,

the mattress
hasn't had sheets—

just us, just detritus, just
knees and suddenly

he snores and passes gas
and is blessedly asleep

only to wake screaming
Turn over turn over, and I

am a chorus
of crickets' legs

rubbing together, of a song
that should be summer,

that should be a song
at all. The word I sing is *Yes*

but the sound just
a slow hot hissing.

Valentine

The heart shape did not start with the heart,
but peepal leaves, silphium, wild carrot—the rounded plants
ancient women found to prevent or end pregnancy. See
also: ivy, fig leaves, damp petals of the water lily. It's not until

crucifixion we get the bloody organ, pierced by a black cross,
a clutched chest the true symbol of devotion, then Luther's Rose,
Danish ballad books, winks at the shape of buttocks
when viewed from behind, private schools with demanding names

like Sacred or Immaculate Heart, a box heavy with chocolates
and rimmed in velvet, children folding red paper in half
with clumsy hands, I Heart NY, i carry your heart with me,
(Everybody's Got a) Hungry Heart, <3, aisles in the drugstore so red

you'd think they were bleeding, which is all ancient women
hoped for each month, not just February, gifting each other
silphium, wild carrot, leaves like paper hearts, what clearer way
to say I love you, I love you, I want you to live.

Defensive Wounds

I can entice you with contusion descriptions:
marigold, plum, lavender heart with butter
petals, thorny ochre crown, freckle-studded,

skin's memory, Girl Scout Badge for Healing.
My husband says *You bruise easily* as if all men
were given the same phrasebook the day hair

darkened their upper lips. The surprise discolorations
of puberty, new patches shrouding the best
body parts in shadow. Suddenly, my skin

was an invitation. No one asks for it. I don't
bruise easily, and I never have. Peony, lemon
peel, bite marks like rubies encircling a center

diamond, cushion cut, pomegranate paws, long
claw marks left in clay—my blood rushed here
to meet you. My blood covered its face with its hands.

Glamping

Full of cracks. Crack-full. On the drive, your neck
looks dry and vampired. Bug bites, blood kisses. I like

your weird knapsack. Where are you taking me,
and what have you brought along. I can see smoke

rising blue on the mountains. They say
you'd have to be crazy to come here at night. Tongue

pond. Inky scream. Every twig a swift
erection beneath our feet. To think

what men must maintain to prove dominion.
Tell me your secret, cracked king. It can't be just

that budget crown. Why have I followed you
here for this gory leaf-peeping. Fuck how alone

you've made us. Fuck the wordless trees. Fuck my own
compliant mug. Fuck my bored feet, my reasons

even I can't explain because I was not taught
a vocabulary that might free me. Most of all: Fuck

this dark tent, this useless hot plate. Men don't bring
women to the woods to feed them.

The Natural World

Why did he like them
so much, these outside
fucks? We couldn't
stroll a city block
without him clocking
every caverned alley, nor
could we enjoy nature
without him begging me
to lie down in the grass
in the exact outline
of his shadow. Once,
there were bison
just inches from us. (I
have written of this before,
and who wouldn't revisit
the image?). They smelled
mangy and milky
like him, like his
beard, like my body
when he was done. What
was he hoping for?
We all understand
the specifics, but I think
he needed a release
from fear, a brave ecstasy
in the valley, and maybe
a cave to pretend
to retreat to—yes,
he said he wanted me,
but really, I was just
a horse he rode toward
some receding sunset,
some gold horizon he thought

he saw once, but at least
he kept trying
to reach it, at least
I was a good horse.

II.

Language does not heal terror, and if it brings us closer to imagining the sufferer's experience, this too does not necessarily make us feel greater compassion, but a desire for further sensation.

—Paisley Rekdal

Gather

Shouldn't a probation officer know? Your probation officer calls, asks if I still live with you. I'm afraid of your cop friends. Nightmares. Therapy. A new boyfriend. Good dreams where I don't want to wake up because I like being with you again. I move to Texas. You plead guilty. They deem you dangerous. Something called a dangerousness hearing, which seems too obvious a title for a legal proceeding. I go home to my mother's. The arraignment. X-rays. The officer taking pictures of my left thigh, hands, torso, face. Sirens. The hard hotel carpet. You chasing me down the dark street. The fight at the bar. Things will be okay. Your tongue so deep in my mouth my sternum throbs. I say *Hi rabbits*. In our backyard, rabbits. We make sorry love for hours. I pack my bags, but you beg me to stay. You seem to be losing touch with reality or maybe it's me. Weeks in the brutal snow and sorrow at your childhood home. The funeral. Christmas. Your mother dies. This is what I want you to say. You tell me I have to live with you again. Blood in my hair. My thirtieth birthday you throw me against a brick wall. New York. Sex in damp motel rooms. June and July spent driving across the country. I move out, barely. A broken tooth. California. Blame. My small clothes hanging next to yours in the closet like silenced children. Up all night reading to each other. Larry Levis. Cheeks and chin always pink from your rough beard. You've never had them before. I make you lentils. You say *Come see me*. You call on your layover. Wiping my wet face in Terminal B. You are the last person to get on the plane. We say this is something. We say this might be something. We spend ten days in bed. I tell you *Yes but maybe not the way you think*. You ask if I believe in God. I crawl on top of you. In the dark woods, you kiss me. You say *Wanna get out of here*. We meet eyes on a foggy summer porch. I have a gin and tonic. I put on a red dress.

Training

Joy to you! We've won.

—Pheidippides

I run on Tuesdays, Wednesdays, always
Saturdays, when the press of the day ahead
lessens. I run with my headphones

on low so I'll know when a man
approaches. I keep my pace steady, try
to keep my breath slow when the hushed car

rolls slowly beside me. For miles, my eyes
are horse not human, turning side
and more side to catch first what is trying

to catch me. I wish to run alone, to hold
the forest fog against me like a friend, I wish
to lose myself but not be lost. I am never

alone. I run with the men and their own
rhythmic breath, their own desire
to feel and feel better, to fight

their own sense of oblivion. The men climb
the trees, crowd paved streets, they lower
their hat brims at each lamplit corner. Do

they see I run with ghosts? Do they see
the fog of bodies tugging me like a draft?
We are all ambitious interns, smiling

undergrads, fit investment bankers
whose history of running may end up
helping save us. We are all newly

engaged, disappointed with our difficult
fathers, we all love the bright gloss
of the city at night. We keep training

for some future race, spectral
relay team, silenced cheering section.
Do the men hear our collective panting

and mistake it? Let there be no further
misunderstanding: We are heralds,
hemerodromes, knowingly awaiting

the morning we will be asked
to run for days, naked, tasked only
with delivering the news we were given.

American Road Trip

From Oakland to nowhere. Salt flats,
Badlands, Devil's Tower swelling

before us then receding in the rearview
like a warning. Bob Barker

Born Here. The rope of your arm
around my shoulders throughout

the informational video for Crazy Horse.
You always told me safety

meant seeing all the way
to the horizon unobstructed,

and who would know better than you
the parameters of a strong defense?

Your heart rate slowed when we were
alone in a field in Wyoming but really

I was alone, you on top of me like
a question I still haven't answered. The bison

lumbering closer—rank, irritated—
their hooves trembling the earth

beneath us, my body shifting in between
like a fault line. Turning my face

away from your turned-away face, a frenzy
of eyes, searching the blank horizon.

Summons

I used to call boys
        after my parents
passed out,
        my lethal friend Meredith
daring me
        to phone Patrick or Michael
and ask what they were wearing.
        One boy, Joey,
played piano
        for me for hours,
while I lay with the phone tucked
        like a pillow
against my red-hot ear.
        I called my mother from college
nightly to try and detect
        how drunk she might be,
whether or not she loved me
        more from longing.
One blizzard, she let me
        watch *When a Stranger Calls*, the sick
moment when the police at last
        call Carol Kane back,
cry *The call is coming*
        from inside the house.
Ted Kennedy called
        Mary Jo Kopechne
baby and *sugar lips*, likely
        the same names he used
on his wife because
        bad love is always
lazy. That night,
        the police stayed
uncalled. I've called
        the police

twice: once when I saw
     a drunk I thought was dead
on 14th Street, once from the floor
     of a seaside B&B
after you'd held your boot
     so hard against my throat the tread
left behind its diamonds. The cops
     could've dusted my neck
like dirt. When you
     called me from
the seaside jail, you said *Baby*
     they're recording us
which I much later understood
     as a plea
not to incriminate you further.
     I can't remember
what I did say
     instead, I can't remember
how I responded
     when either dispatcher
asked flatly *What*
     is your emergency. On TV,
in these recordings,
     the caller is always
upset. When Watson
     answered the first phone call,
Bell didn't celebrate,
     instead he beckoned
his friend, said *Come here I need you.*

Panic Aubade

There are so many things I want to tell you. I have a kitten
who was weaned too early so he kneads my hair nightly
in search of a nipple. I wake with paw marks like hickeys
printing the wet beach of my neck. My neighbors have
been fighting in their driveway. Fighting might not be
the word. Shucking? Deboning? She calls him *out of control,*
and I have forgotten the math for how finite a resource
control can be; he calls her *drunk* and *bitch,* and I begin
to remember. When the man peels out in his truck, I duck,
crouching near the ground, near my kitten who
seems pleased to have my animalness confirmed,
who sometimes kneads my hair so hard he knots it
around his small paw and begins to thrash and mew,
having hewn himself too tightly to the thing he thought
might feed him. Did I tell you yet about the bread knife
in my nightstand? As if I could lift it against you when
you come for me, as if its serrations were a threat to anything
but sourdough. I work to unbraid my hair from my kitten's
wrist. He cannot tell me why he will never stop
being afraid, no matter how many times or how silently
I do this. Into this darkness, my neighbor's headlights surge.

Grief Bacon

The sky is very blue today, and wide. I wish I'd been the first

to evaluate this vision and say *blue*, the first to stretch my arms

as far apart as possible, tugging my beautiful shoulders

from their globular sockets, inventing a whistle that sounded,

for the first time, like *wide*. Longer than the sky

have things been happening that we have yet

to name. We play at piracy, language pillaging, are tickled

over *hygge*, understand the parameters of *schlemiel*

and *schlimazel* but can't define where the mind goes when the body stops

resisting, what the horizon looks like there, how

the casual observer could mistake the vacancy

in a face for tolerance if anyone took

a picture of this, which he did, without asking, just the bright sudden flash

and the second and third sudden flash, the sheets and walls cast

to oblivion by his handheld coroner's lamp. In German, they call weight

gained from emotional eating *kummerspeck*, which is the sum of grief + bacon. So perhaps it's a matter of simple

addition: the sky is *bluewide*, the woman

is *heregone*, every room

she walks into is *monsterfull, allstaring.*

Procedure

The last time I'll ever see you, a man
has his gentle hand on the back of your head

so you don't hit it as he guides you into
a squad car. I am in the street, shoeless,

braced against the seaside wind—a hot,
black magnolia blooming

on my face—bathed in a rush
of red lights. Another man in a cop

costume says *You're shaking*,
and guides me back inside. He is

tall, square jawed, starring in his own
hero film. It's three a.m. I ask

if we can undo this. He says
It's already done. My body is wild

enough that he touches me,
which I assume

is not allowed,
but still welcome. You would

hate that. He says *I'm going through
a separation, too* as if that is what just

happened, as if one tall man were not
removed only to be replaced with

another. As if *Hey, we're both*
on the market now. Do I like a man

in uniform? Where you stood over me
moments ago, he now kneels, a new

sheriff in town. Where you stared, he
assesses, asks if I have any injuries

he cannot see. Where your hands
landed (my stomach, left hip

bone), his hands go. Taking my wrist,
he guides me to stand and says *Steady.*

He tells me I have to take off
my clothes so he

can take my picture.
Everything turns familiar.

Two Truths & a Lie

My uncle used to dress my mother up
in an old white nightgown, paint her skin

sickly and have her lie silent in the attic,
charging the neighborhood kids
a dime to see the dead girl. My mother

was very ill a few years ago, her flesh
damp and malleable as dough. She wanted

the curtains open. She has never
been the same. My mother
has never shot a gun. My mother married

my father on a ski slope in Wyoming
surrounded by strangers. She never said

"I do"; my father said "she does." My mother
and father were married. My father
is married to someone

else, my father is a candle
in every dark room, but he's the one

who's cut the power. *I've come to save you
from what I created.* My mother
is my father, my father is a man

named Matthew, a man named
James, a man named Andrew,

a man named. My name
would have been different
in every way, certainly

less sibilant. My mother is named
after a Mouseketeer. I think your children

should name you, instead.
I would name my mother Citrus,
I would name her Heathcliff, I would name her

Daisy, Windswept, Stanza, Question,
Diana, Hitchhike, Hera, Tolstoy. I would give

my mother a new name
every morning, waking up
near her, the curtains open, seeing in her dawn face

what might happen
that day, who she might like to be.

Path of Totality

Walking back from the Ingles in Hiawassee, Georgia.
Shirtless boys selling celestial
        paraphernalia from the backs of their best friends' Chevys.

                My father lives near here,
I've heard, alone, in a cave or in a field or behind
            someone else's home, but I won't

                call him, wouldn't even know
        his number or the slant
            of his hello. Does he have

an iPhone? Whose picture lights up
the screen when he
        unlocks it? What glasses must he don to look
directly at her?

            I hate to say it but *eclipse* originally meant
                      the abandonment. I'm worried

about aging from too much sun, worried about looking
        any less beautiful the next time I see an old love,
we're all worried
        about going blind even though

            these glasses say *NASA*, say
ISO Certified, but when the low mountains

        are nighttime still and the crickets, confused,

start chirping, and I'm so bourbon soaked
and daytime cold I think maybe
I should call my father, maybe aging is worth

the warmth, maybe it's better to go blind all at once
and from something beautiful.

Fire Breathing

Come not between the dragon and his wrath…
I loved her most.

—King Lear

What do you want me
to say, and how? I call you
Matthew, I call you

Titus, I call out the sound
you stitched in me, sharp
bell in the dry dark

of sudden waking.
You chambered me
as a child, roped

my tongue in riddle.
How could I not go now
toward the bonfire casting

its auburn in the slate field?
I dream you on the flame's
far side, palms turned skyward

in supplication, a match
balanced in your bared
teeth. If I callow myself

to silence, I can hear
the hum of your leftover
devotion, strumming behind

the blaze's husky rumble. It is
the finger you are always curling
to me, the song that once put me

to sleep. How do you keep
your love so hushed? You gave me
a name, now say it.

Elegy for My Mother's Boyfriend

after James Kimbrell

I don't think you're dead,
yet, Randy. I bet you're still
coaching tennis at the club,
watching the best-looking
moms chase their youth

around the clay courts
in expensive pleats. I do
think you loved my mother
for a minute, slouching
around our detonated

home as if you had not
been one of the many fingers
on the trigger. Having taught
me how to palm a racket, how
to watch for the exact moment

the ball begins to drop, tennis
court kairos, cool fall afternoons
before you complained there
was no more coffee and why
would a sixteen-year-old

drink caffeine anyway, before
my mother went so mute
with defeat that she let you
stomp around her daughters,
bloated and boxered, as if
you'd been a champion once.

Summering

I dress like Redford in *The Way We Were*:
tennis sweaters and tight pants, a mouth you can't quite
get a hold of. There is white noise
in my narrowness. I am implacable and American.

They say *old money* is back in. I keep menstruating
all over the linen. Once a month, I get a little silly
in a black tuxedo. You know that Garbo hid
at the end. She called *Two-Faced Woman* her "grave."

It wasn't me who said the word *enemy*, I'm only here
to trouble the service line. My backhand is smooth
and silent, my face a clean-cut plunder.

Hamartia

I.

Racine said the failings of love are real failings.
Excessive susceptibility to sexual feelings is an example
of a failure of love.

So too loving one's father or mother too much.
The azalea of her hair.
The grand piano of his beard.

II.

It should not be understood as a collapse of morality.
A misunderstanding. A farce
starring my dragged heart.

Who will care for me, now? The audience,
crying out, warning me beneath
which bedsheets lurks the monster.

III.

Anagnorisis is a comatose word
for the moment of discovery. The curtain
pulled, first fires set. Enter my half-dressed

mother, father, brother, lover. Each
can be told from each by the choice
of costume, weapon, subtle changes in the lighting scheme.

IV.
Would that we could script what we love and how much,
I'd have written: planetarium, hammerhead, ruby-studded
teacups, and as little

as possible. No one wants to watch the play where the heroine
coughs for the entire final act. What doesn't kill you
assumes you're already dead.

III.

We might learn to let ourselves bump into things; not to withdraw in anticipation of violence.

—Sara Ahmed

Mandatory Reporter

Click-click, click-click, he flicks
his pen rhythmically. On the wall behind him,

the red university logo
hovers like a crucifix.

His vest is fleece, oatmeal-
toned, as are his cheeks. Even his lips

are old biscuits. He licks his thumb
and draws it to his documents

while I wonder what he does for fun.
Can you tell me a little about

your relationship to him? he asks, as if
the relationship was ever mine. All I kept

was the secret. Why
did I grow my hair this long? It's hot,

and hard to manage.
His damp thumb clicks

the pen quicker. *I mean*—he leans
against my silence—*Was he ever*

attracted to you? And how could you tell?
The corners of his biscuit mouth

look buttered. Who made him
breakfast, I wonder. Was he alone

when he woke? I know
I need to speak, but if I do, he will see

my tongue. Finally, I say
Can you be more specific? His pen's

wicked red metronome stills.
Can you ask me, for instance:

Did he rest a dry hand on your knee
under any crowded tables?

Were you startled
by how certainly he gripped it?

Did you wear bare legs in some
goosebumped hope for this exact preamble?

Did he show up at your door and lift
a quiet finger to his lips?

Did he tell you to change
your dress?

Did he cut off
your circulation?

Did he name you muse, glory, lighthouse,
energy, star, dream of his boyhood?

Did you feel
like an apparition?

Like more or less
of a success?

Did he make you shred
the condom despite your swollen gums?

Do you have evidence
of the destruction of evidence?

What did he like most, and how did it feel
to be the one giving it to him?

The long table between us
is so clean, I can't imagine

another woman has ever sat here
answering to him.

What does he ask me, actually?
I think we have been in this

beige room for days. Silence
drools between us.

In another state, my mother
sets a pot on the stove's blue flame.

I'm just following the mandate, he says.
Funny word, I say, *man-date?* He looks at me, his vest

looks at me, as if humor is not something
I have earned. *Do you have enough,*

I say, but now he's writing
something quickly. The school logo moves

like a sun across the sky
of this room's dismissals.

I am a chair in which
he has made himself

comfortable. I am asking
about procedure when the word

I want is mercy.
Can I go now, I ask, and, if so, to where?

The morning after,
I wake in the dark

to read books that haven't touched me
in years. Old marginalia written

by some silly muse, stupid star, dream
of my own childhood. I flush

at her scribbled intimacies.
I was young, and wanted

to take myself seriously. By the time
I come to the line:

At sea I woke in chills, I shivered in the wake of your pleasure,

the sun has risen. It cheers
the windows, the page, my old

pulsing performance. Daylight
demands a different life

than the one I'm capable of. He gave me
this book, he still lives

just down the street. If I spit, it might hit
his kitchen window, where she

is undoubtedly standing, kneading bread
for their children. He would recognize

the spit as mine. He is close enough to hear
my tongue gathering itself

against my gums, so I consider
what sounds I should make

before I make them: He liked
the brush's whoosh

through my hair, a fireplace
grinning to life. He loved the soft

suction of the bathtub faucet turning
off, and my deadbolt's slither

as it slid into place—another system
meant to keep us safe. Best, he liked

the silence before
the sound, my mouth opening

beneath his grip. I know
what he expected,

in those moments,
and it wasn't this.

Internalized

Elizabeth Wurtzel once tried
to soothe me, said it was good to live

the forever bachelorette life.
Why wouldn't I believe her? Maybe

it was the drop of blood
on her fur coat or the fact

of her fur coat at all, or maybe
the speckled chestnut roots spilling

like sludge into her blonde hair.
What's that phrase they say? *It me.*

I wonder if one day I'll be a woman
interviewers ask only about a man

I fucked for a few years
years ago. Maybe fewer

than a few years. But who
can help it? I still love

his name in the room.
Who can help?

I don't eat meat and I would *never*
wear fur. The windows here

are thumb-smudged and struck
with Valentine's glitter. Don't act

as if you've never heard a ghost
wailing from the cellar

and simply turned the sitcom
volume up—Monica Geller's

tirade on tidiness
an aria against remembrance.

Dental Office Erotica

Dr. Joel lowers me
before him. My body
unfolding with the mechanical chair, the whirr

both ominous and pleasant.
He keeps calling me
young lady, and I'm pleased

to have fooled him twice.
The hygienist sucks my spit
and blood as Dr. Joel thrusts

a separator into the not-numb-enough
corner of my jaw. The plastic is stiff
and takes its work seriously. I hope my lips

look more luscious
from the pressure of the spread.
I hope Dr. Joel is quietly humming

"Build Me Up Buttercup" to keep himself
from becoming erect.
Scrubs are unforgiving

to the lustful. My hair
splayed on the green
pleather, he peers

into the cavity he's filling,
glances back at the X-ray behind me.
Your mouth he says

has sustained considerable trauma.
I goggle a sound,
but I've lost him. I wink

and the hygienist asks
if she should move the light.
I'm going to numb you Dr. Joel says, touching

my shoulder, *a little more.* I try to smile against
the syringe, against the light. I try
to arch my back in the chair

the way I remember
sometimes works. Dr. Joel says *Don't worry.*
Dr. Joel says *Now a little pinch.*

Selling Sunset

These walls are made of kitten fur.

Every time you take a bath, the moon sets in the pink sink.

Don't let the faucet water touch any exposed skin.

Warren G. Harding drooled, napped, and died in this bed.

There was basically no blood.

When the lighthouse blinks on, you can see the ships lost at sea.

That spot on the water you can't look away from?

She drowned while her husband watched.

Down this flight here, we have a solarium that doubles as obelisk.

The attire is midnight snack.

The cuisine is a jar of maraschino cherries, but you only eat the syrup that suspends them.

These mossy breadcrumbs chart a path to the private beach.

We've kept the tide static for you.

It sounds almost like birdsong, but we haven't determined who's singing.

Morning isn't coming.

Your heart will never recover.

Sermon

can I call myself secular if
after Christmas winter kneels
before me like a penitent I am

melancholy's high priest
the pastor of slipping on black ice
apples from my paper bag tumbling

down Hudson wailing
freedom! freedom!
I crawl with broken

ankle up the mountain
of my walk-up begging
a parishioner to pack ice

against my turned bones
in the city we call
the worst months of wet snow

Smebruary and *Smarch* so now I set
my calendar to this system aging
only every other year renaming

myself *Smessica* so no one will remember
how pretty I was when first I fell how
overnight I turned to gutter

sludge but also we together
forget how much
Smessica loved you

how deftly she gave you
away then quickly filled
the pews of her bedroom with men gave them

shelter and bloodwine and a lecture
on piety while pulling
her layers off like Christmas

wrapping sweating
from the pulpit headboard crying
in tongues vowing

that you shall call my name and you
shall be saved and you shall
know god by my tears by my hot love alone

Psalm for Superbowl Sunday

Jesus rose on a Sunday, we suppose. Was he asleep,
again, by nightfall? Some say he stayed for forty days
and celebrated. Who knows if ghosts need their rest—

so often they nap when we're cleaning the kitchen, then
come moaning down the long hall just as we've hit
the opening scene of a sex dream. What makes a man

a ghost and not the second coming? A case,
perhaps, like obscenity: you will know Him
when you see Him. It could also be a question

of lighting, and of who brings whom the news. Today,
we gather in winged consensus and make
our address to God—O, sit for a bit, we know You

are busy, but we've been working hard to be accurate
about sorrow: ailing parents, broadcast death, hearts
that beat too hard when we rise from prayer, and the soft waves

swelling over the beachfront of our brains. We can't read
Your facial expression. Say something, already. The sun
is setting when a woman's low song disrupts

His silence. Turning to her, we glimpse—
for an instant—the sparkled arc of an ass
to crash the heavens. Is it one of us? Are we

that beautiful and dangerous? When did you say, God,
that our suffering could not be solved without you?

The One Where Ross Dates His Student

He visits her dorm room in his professor coat. She squirts
a water balloon in his face. A game with her roommates. I watch
the episode on mute in a mussed hotel bed. I'm trying to write a poem
while trying to look like Rachel Greene. I spent my precious evening
hours with a man, courting his hard thrall. He watched the episode
I played for him—The One Where I Know What You Like—on mute.
Rachel Greene stalked the edges of the scene. Ross Geller murmured
he was serious about this student, that she was The One. I spent
my precious evening hours investing in returns that won't come.

Fall on Your Knees

Please host a few funerals
for these little deaths I keep
dying. Veil your lashes
with lace, veil your gaze
in damp lashes. We all look
better a little sad. It was you
who named the act *sacred*. The word
persuades when you are the one
saying it. A forked tongue lapping
at tongues. It was just
a tree. My teeth
barely denting the fluffy
red flesh. Pass the coffer.
Bow your head. The altar
creates the saint.

Doctor's Orders

step on a slug and you'll be nasty
for nine days, don't let anyone
sweep under your feet or you'll

never marry, hold your breath
over bridges, hold your breath
past the graveyard, hold your

breath, hold steady, hold
your own, stay in your mother's
bed, hold the perfume

of her milk in your lungs, sleep
on your stomach so your lungs
don't fill with fluid

and crush you, hold your breath
past that man, suck in
your stomach so your dress

will look better, hold
your breath when you kiss, hold
your tongue when he asks

for an answer, let the bed
you sleep on carry you back
to your mother, back to her milk,

your lungs splitting open to let in
her light, to inhale the honey, you'll do
anything to save her, to save this,

to be the one holding
your breath, not the grave
no one breathes on when they pass

She's a ten but she

eats raw bacon with her bare hands keeps
her fingernails long until they break off naturally

in the course of digging shallow graves for her dolls
her eyeless gutless hottie dolls all of which

were gifts she's a ten but these are her
friends she's a ten but she licks

her father's headstone each time she visits uses
the spit to affix flower petals in the shape of a *D*

to the granite or is it marble she's a ten but she can't
tell the difference she can't sit at a table

long enough for the drinks to come even if you've agreed
to pay the first check and the check that comes

after you keep slipping your hand into your
pocket she's starting to think there's more in there

than money she's starting to think the white linens
are swaddles and she should wrap you up

in the breadbasket leave you outside the fire
station she's a ten but she has options she's a ten

but her missing teeth are on a string around
your neck she's a ten but the only university

she attended was the school of retrieval the art
of crepuscular stealth how to mime effectiveness

in ten easy steps she pinches her cheeks until her blood
pinks them she rims her eyes in wet soil this is what

they would have wanted and just because you've never
heard her say *yes* doesn't mean she doesn't know how

DARVO

Sounds like *parvo*, sounds like don't
let the puppy loose if he hasn't
had his shots. Sounds like

Bravo!, like retreating
backstage after the second
encore, like he's waiting

in your dressing room and not
clapping. Sounds like *Darwin*, like
survival of the fittest, like *Mr. Darcy*,

like enemies to lovers, like Austen
thought you could love someone
into tenderness, like "...in every

disposition a tendency to some
particular evil—a natural
defect." Sounds like *dashcam*, like

doorway, like *bard*, like *darnedest*,
like the flabbiest acronym, though
it was intended to tighten

the duration of comprehension.
It's a mnemonic, *darling*. Don't you
remember? Understand. Quicker.

IV.

Humans in love are terrible.
—Anne Carson

Lady Smith

I never thought I'd love a man
with a room full of skulls, a deer's ear fur
still clinging where he hasn't finished

cleaning out the sockets. He tells me when
he killed this one, and how. Amazing
how many methods there are

for only one outcome. He lifts a gun—longer
than a cobra, blacker than burnt
shrapnel—from its glass case. *This one,*

he says, *was my father's.* His arms strain
with beloved weight, the weapon
as heavy as me in the morning

when I want him to take me
home and he won't. *This one,*
he says, pulling a petite piece

of chrome from the bottom drawer,
is for you. His first gift. My West Texas
protection. My pink handle with grooves

designed for smaller hands. If
I hold my fist just loose
enough, barely tickle the delicate

trigger, the grip fits perfectly, my Lady Smith
dangling like an afterthought
from the flimsy of my wrist. I move it

against his chest. I draw
a heart on his sternum
with its tip. *Yes*, he smiles, *you get it.*

My Love and I Are Inventing a Country

In South Dakota or Minnesota, they mistakenly
upgraded us to a suite. We were giddy
with accident, even if the place still reeked
of carpet cleaner and stale humidity. My head
thrown back in the cheap sheets, your head
somewhere between the foot of the bed and me.
We turned out the lights in all three (*three!*)
rooms and watched porn on your
computer screen: petite blonde begging
for a better grade, pigtails and a prep-school
skirt, only the caesarean scar to give her
away. We laughed that we liked it when
the men left on their socks, when the boom
mic dipped into the scene. In the middle
of the night we went for burgers, so juicy
and affordable they were practically free.
You said *you are going to get married*
to me and I, mouthful of grease, said
happily, happily. There was no need
to wait, even for morning, so why did we.

Dark Hollow Falls

for Dean

Late morning and the dark bear
crosses the path not thirty feet
before us—his plush sofa body

wobbling toward a bright flap
of wrapper caught in the brush. I clench
both fists instantly, watching

the bear sniff a straight line
for a Snickers that no longer
exists. Finding the wrapper

empty, will the driven beast
not sate himself on the nearest,
pliant flesh? Perhaps I do not

understand anything
about bears. I have lived a long time
in the city, have barely seen

an *animal* in years, but today I
am with you. I am always lucky
for that, particularly in this

dangerous instance because you
are from Idaho where bears
are bigger than restaurants,

so you hold me and say *Scream,*
start screaming, which seems
wrong, to alert the bear,

but you say *Scream,*
don't make eye contact, just keep
screaming, two behaviors

I have learned well
to perform in tandem. You scream,
too, and hold me while I scream,

pausing to say *It's fine, he doesn't*
want us, but I've never
known a predator

not to want, and I've never known you
not to soothe me even if comfort invites
the lie. Still I scream

enough for the both of us, my bare
summer arms and thighs trembling
at the volume. The bear looks,

and looks, and turns away, ambling deeper
into the forest and you say *Don't move*
too fast, but I've already taken off

at a sprint, still screaming, leaving you
there, on the dirt path, whispering
your sweet safety to no one.

The Standard

In a black bathtub, the water looks black. I swim up to you
as through God's womb, surfacing tongue-first to swallow
the rich dark milk of your gaze. My thirst turns me into a two-
headed beast who can glimpse her own image, her own
certain outcomes, her own slow demise. Tomorrow we'll have
just lush honey residue, sunrise spreading its dry gloom
over our wading limbs. But, for now, our champagne flutes
are nightlights on the tub's lip, your broad chest half
submerged like the moon rising over a lake. Aren't you
worried your camera will get wet, and ruined? Who will save
these fatal moments if it does, who will catch
the petals rippling when your teeth discover my pistil's
limit? Even we were shocked by our own eyes in the dark,
by the camera's clapping flash, and what it captured.

Cocked

I used to think there was nothing better
than making love, nothing better

than watching a face
practiced in the impassive

suddenly race to the cliff's edge, collapse
into the ocean's hot madness. No wonder we give up

so much, so fast. I was raised
to be coy about pleasure, to let it find me

by accident. My expressions
may have been too evident, my ass round and glowing

like a sky with two moons. They say *He should
have known better*—he did, he knew the best.

Retreat

I had a lover in
the woods, his body
slight and shaking.

We dipped ourselves
like fingers into cold
streams and emerged

with something to
taste. One night I bled
all over his sheets but

in the moonlight, through
the window, the red
looked like a map, not

a mistake. The sheets
seemed the deviance,
the glass and wood separating

us from the night the
unnatural—not the air, not
the stream, not the blood.

In daylight we sought
no linen to cover the green
burnt into my back, no

knitted summer shawl
to wrap the wet at
our knees, just

his tentative hands
turning certain, the same
way the moon's

pale silhouette in late
afternoon reminds us
what will shine in full dark.

Fitspo

your hair curlicues into apostrophes
when you sweat as if every exertion
were contraction. we're out running,

hips shifting like parentheses, dripping
exclamation of ponytail. we're panting
in our separate bodies. we stop

to take in the forest, which is quiet
but not still. you wipe your apostrophed
brow. dusk thrills the trees. your

palms, my knees. name
a body part that is not a verb.

Encore

Low flame creeps from the pipe in your loud mouth. The bright
of me recast each day by artificial means: the ashes
from your fire breathing, glare of needy teeth, bared

as if to smile. I shadow-puppet filthily, ballerina backlit by
the hazy spotlight of smoke. As part of the show, I recite
the short list of things that still move me: my youngest sister's

wet eyelashes, a song my mother used to sing in the kitchen
when snipping the ends from roses. *Like a summer*, she
hummed, *with a thousand Julys.* I've given up

on sleep, basking in the glare of exhaustion with you,
your tongue thumping on the floor like a cartoon
wolf. *Ahooga*, you sonuvabitch. *Ahooga*, you perfect

pervert. Now, sit still and stop shaking. Slice me
a mango and watch me eat it. I'll jelly my body in juice
for you, I'll pink and thick and glisten. Hard to say now

who is audience. Something laced, something leather,
something borrowed, something bodice, switchblade
tucked into a garter. This is all to say *yes*—the show

might go on forever, the stars shivering their nervous watch
on us, the angels blushing at the blood we draw, the silent applause
in your burnt mouth when I let you, let you, let you.

Lucid

You hadn't come to find me
in a long time, but I had not
forgotten how it feels when
you do. I dreamt you had become
more fashion-forward,
dispensing of bad khakis
and pilled fleece in favor of bright
banana shoes whose heels were
dewy clusters of grapes. I dreamt
you told me the clothes reflected
your new inner life. I dreamt we worked
suddenly at the same institution
and our colleagues were concerned
for me. I dreamt you hid in classroom
corners beckoning, reminding me of our
most unprofessional secrets. You reached
for me in a bespoke blazer and said
I've changed, your lavender silk shirt
gleaming as it never would have
in our life, your brown eyes soft and pleading
as they sometimes were in our life.
I dreamt you wanted to show me
what you'd saved of mine: a scrap
of paper on which I'd scribbled
a grocery list, a picture of me as
a child at Christmas, a gray
wool scarf I wore even
in summer. You said *Now I understand*
why you were always cold. I was grateful
for the dream, grateful for your new
and impossible haute couture, grateful
for our surprising employment
and proximity. I was grateful

for your gentle admissions,
grateful to be allowed—for
an instant—to love you again.

Bells Will Ring

Medieval knights knelt
as a show of respect.

This history might be helpful
to foreground for the proposer.

I teach my students
to arrange symbols into lines

that transfer feeling. What is the quality
of a knight on bent knee? I teach my students

what to leave out.
Teaching is easier work than, say,

when I was a hostess at
a high-end steakhouse in DC.

All those senators and their similes:
You have an ass like a sunrise

is a more interesting image than many
that have been dripped on my chin.

I tell my students: Kangaroo pouches
are not plush and fuzzy

as cartoons have led us to believe.
We domesticate animals

so they'll die before we do. We say it's good
for our children, to learn.

I tell my students:
Loss is a bedsheet

fluttering on a clothesline in winter.
When we speak of it after,

there might be plot holes.
Milk man, late morning, snowfall, blanc.

Abscess, slapped cheek, cherry bomb, wine.
Queen Victoria was the first

to wear white: silk satin thicker
than bone, a tiara with tips like teeth.

Why Don't We Paint the Town

I married an older man and why? I do not wish
to be alone when they turn the lights on. Perhaps
I've thought too carefully about the overture
and not the coda. I would like, right now, to have lips
so red that even the cheap seats feel kissed. I'm still
pretty with this ghost mouth though. That is okay to say,
okay? I am done with pretending you didn't audition
for this role, that you were even interested
in the play before I was cast. What a waste—
these days of tap dancing away from each other
and back into the eaves. I liked the spotlight I couldn't
see beyond. I liked my tight little costume. I didn't mind
when you asked me what I was afraid of,
what I was willing to do to feel safe.

On Earth

While I held you inside me, your grandfather
died. His body was closer in death than
it had been in his insufficient life. Each time
I wished to hold my father, I pressed my hand
to you, which was also a way of holding
myself. There are so few remedies,

so little to be known. I advance and retreat
based mostly on hope—the hope that what
I reach for is real. I teach my students
to seek for questions instead of answers,
in the hopes I might save them a lifetime
—albeit short—of searching. And you,

child who is answer not question, child
who is full morning, aubade, child whose
response is most often song, I don't ask
if you will live forever because I must live
in the certainty that you will, I must
manufacture an answer despite my best

intellect, I must believe that when I die, you
will still be the sun rising over the earth
each morning, that you will sing
to my students who, surely, will also survive,
eternally seeking questions based on
my excellent, unforgotten tutelage, yes—

in memory I hope to be more certain
and inspiring, because I know that now, when you
cry—set down in your crib, or handed to your father
—it is because you believe this might be
the last time we touch, and I am reminded,
every time, that you might be right.

Acknowledgments

With gratitude to the following places, where poems or versions of these poems have appeared previously:

THE BOILER JOURNAL: "Vow"

Cincinnati Review miCRo: "Path of Totality"

Cincinnati Review: "Training" (reprinted in *Verse Daily*)

Four Way Review: "Summons"

Freshwater Review: "Elegy for My Mother's Boyfriend"

Hayden's Ferry Review: "Valentine"

Hoxie Gorge Review: "Dark Hollow Falls"

Identity Theory: "The Standard," "Why Don't We Paint the Town"

Juked: "Encore"

NELLE: "Internalized," "Cocked"

Rappahannock Review: "Fire Breathing"

The Rumpus: "Things People Say to Me After"

Salt Hill: "Scold's Bridle" (reprinted in *VerseDaily*)

The Shallow Ends: "Two Truths & a Lie"

The Shore: "Retreat"

Southern Indiana Review: "Luster," "Gather"

32 Poems: "Lady Smith"

Waxwing Literary Journal: "My Love and I Are Inventing a Country," "No Other Appetite," "Ode to StairMaster"

To the team at UA Press—Mary Biddinger, Amy Freels, and Brittany LaPointe. Thank you for choosing this book and for shepherding me through the process.

To Sandra Beasley, for selecting my manuscript and helping guide it into a more fully realized version.

To the Sewanee Writers' Conference, for their ongoing support over the years.

To Vermont Studio Center, for the month spent writing.

To the creative writing departments at The New School and at Texas Tech University, particularly Craig Morgan Teicher, David Lehman, Leslie Jill Patterson, and Katie Cortese.

To my dissertation director, friend, neighbor, colleague, and mentor Curtis Bauer.

To my forever crew—Ellie Birch, Brianna Carbonneau, Lauren Loucas, Jessica Jones, Kathleen Doyle Anderson, Hannah Byam, Caitlin Wall, Claire Krawszcyn, Molly Nelson, Mark Loucas, and Will Anderson.

To people who helped with these poems along the way—Chen Chen, Sarah Viren, Sara Sams, Bojan Louis, Chelsea Whitton, Brenda Shaughnessy, Mag Gabbert, Kenna Neitch, Jess Krause, Marc DeHate, Elissa Zellinger, Callie Kostelich, Elizabeth Sharp, Don Lavigne, Dana Weiser, Josh Luckenbach, Maddie Ward, Jessica Gross, Matt Hunter, Scott Weedon, Aaron Braver, Ryan Hackenbracht, Caleb Braun, Corey Van Landingham, Christine Adams, Diana Khoi Nguyen, Jasmine Epstein, William Brown, and Jennifer Popa.

To Tomás Morín for years of long, uncensored talks.

To Evan Dean for keeping me alive.

To my late father Matthew, and to my older siblings Matt and Mary Katherine. To Amanda and Alex and Andy.

To Claire and Genevieve, because I could never love anyone as I love my seesters.

To Jim, for all you did for me, for teaching me a career was a life, too.

To Phyllis Ann, for the poems you gave me.

To Cheryl Ann, the story of my life is the story of your life.

To Mike, for the child we have, for the life we built and are still building.

And to Tommy, who made me fearless.

Jess Smith is the author of *Lady Smith*, the winner of the 2023 Akron Poetry Prize. Originally from Georgia, she is currently an assistant professor of practice at Texas Tech University, where she also directs the MFA in creative writing.